PEOPLE
YOU GOTTA MEET
BEFORE YOU
GROW UP

Get to Know the Movers and Shakers,
Heroes and Hotshots in Your Hometown

· Joe Rhatigan ·

imagine! Publishing

An Imagine Book
Published by Charlesbridge.
85 Main Street, Watertown, MA 02472
(617) 926-0329
www.charlesbridge.com

Library of Congress Cataloging-in-Publication Data

Rhatigan, Joe.
 People you gotta meet before you grow-up : get to know the movers and shakers, heroes and hot shots in your hometown / by Joe Rhatigan.
      pages cm.
 "An Imagine book."
 Includes bibliographical references and index.
 ISBN 978-1-62354-004-3 (alk. paper)
 1. Civic leaders—Juvenile literature. 2. Interviewing—Juvenile literature. 3. Community development—Juvenile literature. 4. Community life—Juvenile literature. I. Title.
 HN49.C6R495 2013
 307.77--dc23
                                              2013015435

2 4 6 8 10 9 7 5 3 1

For information about custom editions, special sales, premium and corporate purchases, please contact Charlesbridge Publishing at specialsales@charlesbridge.com

To Beth ... I'm sure glad I met you!—J.R.

Contents

Introduction

Have you ever met someone famous? A celebrity athlete or a movie star, perhaps? How about a reality TV show contestant, a senator, or a musician? We're fascinated with these people. We know their faces, want their autographs, and would love to meet them. They're the movers and shakers of the world! Unfortunately, the chances of spending time with them are slim. They live in completely different

How do famous people ever get anything done?

worlds, and although they have many fans, very few can get close enough to even ask a question.

Fortunately, you can meet people who are just as interesting and fascinating as those you see on TV or in magazines simply by walking out your door—the movers and shakers of your own neighborhood, community, town, or city. These people make things happen, keep us safe, entertain us, and help us, all without headlines and paparazzi. And this book is going to help you meet them! So even though your chances of meeting LeBron James aren't all that great, you can meet a high school athlete who's about to go off to college on a sports scholarship. Wishing you could have dinner with the president? Good luck with that! But hey, who's running your town or city? There's a good chance you could meet them and even tour their office. These world-changers stand in line next to you at the grocery store, no bodyguards needed. But they change the world just like their famous cohorts do.

How This Book Works

Each section of *People You Gotta Meet* identifies and describes a particular person who would be cool to meet.

- **Strategies** gives you ideas for how to go about meeting this person.
- **Ask Away** provides questions you can ask when you do meet.
- **Some Famous . . .** introduces you to some famous folks to look up.
- **Check It Out** starts off your Internet search for more information about the job or type of person you're reading about.

You'll also find lots of fun facts, interesting tidbits, inspiring quotes, fascinating profiles, and Q&As with interesting people I know or have met while writing this book.

The people you'll meet through the following pages are working to make positive changes in the part of the world you call home. And it is my hope that spending some time with these difference-makers will inspire you to become one as well.

Before You Begin Your Journey

This book is about being curious about people in your community and finding out more about them. This section will give you some ideas on how to meet these people and what to do once you find them!

Reasons to Meet Interesting People

• You want to write an article for the school newspaper or your local newspaper.
• You're interested in their career or life choices.
• You're curious and inquisitive.
• You want to create a video of interesting people.
• You're looking for a new hobby or interest.
• You're passionate about something and want to meet people who share in this passion.

Use Your Kid-ness

Here's a secret that will help you out in life (at least until you're an adult): Grown-ups are impressed with kids who take initiative, ask questions, and otherwise seek knowledge or assistance. Being an inquisitive and interesting kid might get you a behind-the-scenes interview with an interesting person faster than any adult could. So use your kid-ness to your advantage! Here's how:

• When contacting someone, always state your name, how old you are, and what school you go to.
• Don't be afraid to ask for a meeting or an interview. When doing so, tell the person why you'd like to meet with them. Express your interest in what they do and your desire to learn more.

- Do your research before the meeting. For example, if you're meeting a dog trainer, read about his or her business online and brush up on some dog-training techniques beforehand.
- Have questions ready, and don't be afraid to refer to your notes.
- Dress for success. This doesn't mean wearing a stiff suit or a blouse and skirt—just something appropriate and neat.
- Be polite and say "please" and "thank you."
- Make eye contact when talking and listening.
- Don't be afraid to show people how smart you are.
- Don't worry if you're nervous. Remember to breathe. You can even admit that you're nervous! The adult will probably try to put you at ease.
- Be yourself and let your natural curiosity guide you.
- If you're shy, don't pretend you're not. Again, be yourself!
- Write and send out thank-you notes afterward.

Overall Strategies

Nice to meet you!

- No matter which strategies in this book you use, make sure your parents know what you're doing first. Don't attempt to meet people without your parents' knowledge. Do not contact anyone via phone, e-mail, or social media without first talking about what you're planning on doing with a parent. Some of the people you'll meet will be strangers, while others will be neighbors, family members, teachers, and friends. No matter who they are, make sure they know your parents are

involved in your mission. Give them a parent's e-mail address or phone number when first contacting them so they can check in with your mom or dad before talking with you.

- When researching the movers and shakers in your community, ask the people you know first: parents, teachers, friends, neighbors, scout leaders, doctors, etc.
- Many towns have free weekly newspapers that are great resources for finding out what's going on in and around town.
- Ask librarians for help (see page 66).
- You can meet the movers and shakers at your school, their office, your home (invite them to dinner!), or a public place, such as a coffee shop.
- Turn your conversations into articles for the school newspaper or even your local newspaper.
- Start a community blog highlighting all the fascinating people you meet.
- Create a podcast featuring your recorded interviews.
- Create a TV news program for your school and invite community members onto your show for interviews. Post the videos on YouTube or show them in class.

Secrets to Conducting Good Interviews

- Find out all about the person you're interviewing and what he does for a living. That means researching, reading articles, and asking around.
- Make sure you have a list of at least ten to fifteen questions prepared ahead of time. The questions shouldn't be able to be answered with a simple yes or no, and the more specific the question, the better.
- Don't be afraid to ask unscripted questions as they arise.
- Bring at least two pens, a notepad, and a recording device (if you have one) to the interview. (Many smartphones have voice-recording capacity.)
- If you plan on recording your conversation, ask permission to use the recording device beforehand. Take notes even if you are recording the conversation.
- Ask follow-up questions, especially if you don't understand something.
- Write down everything you remember about your interview as soon as possible. The longer you wait, the more you'll forget.

Check It Out

How to conduct an interview: *bit.ly/GK1AQv*
Great questions to ask: *bit.ly/ZS8CLN*

GO TO THE SOURCE
You Gotta Meet a Farmer!

The next time you go to the grocery store, take a close look at the fruits and vegetables in the produce section. Many of the items will have stickers on them telling you where they came from: Mexico, California, Florida, the Midwest . . . But even if you live in any of those places, you'd have a hard time meeting the people who grew that food, because most of it is now grown by large corporations. Sure, farmers still do the work, but it's not like the storybooks say it is, and most of these farms are not open to visitors.

However, there are still thousands of small family-run farms in the United States, producing veggies, fruit, dairy, and meat for stores and restaurants. These are the farmers you have to meet. Their food is produced nearby, so it doesn't have to travel that far to get to your kitchen. That means the food is fresher and more healthful for you. Since their farms are close to you, it's easy to get to

SUPPORT YOUR
LOCAL FARMERS

them. Many of these farmers practice sustainable agriculture—growing and producing food while taking the environment into consideration—which is an added bonus.

Strategies

- Look for produce, meat, and dairy with "Locally Grown" stickers. Some will mention the farm and may even provide a website. Research the farm and e-mail them asking for a personal or school visit.
- Visit farmers' markets, which are like flea markets for local produce. Interview one or more farmers, or, if they're busy, ask for a follow-up interview over the phone, via e-mail, or at their farm.
- Read up on the locally grown movement and let these farmers know you're a "locavore," which is the name given to people who try to buy only local foods.
- Check out a Farm to School program near you.
- Visit a pick-your-own fruit farm.

Ask Away

- What does your farm grow/produce?
- Where does your food end up?
- How is your farm sustainable?
- What's your favorite vegetable? Least favorite?
- What time do you have to get up in the morning?
- How can I become a farmer?

Check It Out

A blog about food and farmers:
bit.ly/10ddOXM

The USDA's Farm Service Agency:
1.usa.gov/cnHJTG

Agriculture activities: *bit.ly/14GuT0g*

National Farm to School Network:
www.farmtoschool.org

SOME FAMOUS
FARMERS—LOOK 'EM UP

JOEL SALATIN
THOMAS JEFFERSON
GEORGE WASHINGTON CARVER
BOB EVANS

"From breakfast, or noon at the latest, to dinner, I am mostly on horseback, attending to my farm or other concerns, which I find healthful to my body, mind, and affairs." —Thomas Jefferson

Top Crops Farmers Grow in the U.S.

- corn
- soybeans
- hay
- wheat
- cotton
- sorghum
- rice

NOT ALL WHO WANDER ARE LOST
You Gotta Meet a Traveler!

Chances are you haven't been to too many places around the world yet. Perhaps you haven't even traveled more than a hundred miles from your home and may not even know to dream of faraway places and exotic locales. Getting to know someone who has can change all that. People travel for many reasons, including vacations, work, visiting family and friends, service work, or just because they like it so much that they find a way to do it as often as possible. You may not catch the "travel bug" getting to know someone who has seen the world, but you will learn more about this incredibly diverse planet and the people who call it home.

Strategies

- Local organizations, libraries, or schools may ask someone who has traveled extensively to come in and share their experiences. They may bring photos, videos, and other mementos of their excursions.
- When asking questions, ask about more than the sights. What about the smells, tastes, textures, and sounds?

Ask Away

- What's the strangest thing you've ever eaten?
- Where do you suggest a future world traveler visit first?
- How many countries have you visited?
- Do you ever miss home?

SOME FAMOUS TRAVELERS

FREYA STARK
BILL BRYSON
MARTIN AND OSA JOHNSON
NELLIE BLY

Check It Out

The world's most recognized student traveler program: peopletopeople.com

Another traveling program for students: www.wheretherebedragons.com

An example of a travelers' meet-up website: www.meetup.com/sanfranciscoworldtravelers

National Geographic's Travel Photos: on.natgeo.com/9K8PTI

Rolf Potts's No Baggage Challenge: www.rtwblog.com

"To awaken alone in a strange town is one of the pleasantest sensations in the world."—Freya Stark

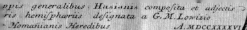

In 2010, travel writer Rolf Potts went on a six-week tour of the world, taking only what he could fit in his pockets. No baggage allowed! He visited twelve countries on five continents carrying only a few items, including a collapsible toothbrush, deodorant, passport, iPod, and some clothing.

Ralph Potts in Ethiopia

18

KAYLEIGH RHATIGAN
(THIS AUTHOR'S DAUGHTER!) IS A TRAVELER

Kayleigh Rhatigan is a sophomore in high school, but when she was in eighth grade, she and several classmates went on a once-in-a-lifetime trip to Cambodia. She's saving her money so it isn't her last trip!

Q: Describe the trip you went on.

A: I went on a nine-day trip to Cambodia. My teachers Kathy Millar and Jason Carter planned it, and we went with a tour group called PEPY (Protect the Earth, Protect Yourself) that focuses on improving education and the environment in Cambodia. We got to go to the usual tourist destinations, like the capital, Phnom Penh, and the ancient temples of Angkor Wat, but we also got to visit some cool NGOs (nongovernmental organizations) and a school.

Q: What memory sticks with you the most?

A: I remember vividly how weird it was right after we had landed in Cambodia and I was still getting over the shock of being in a completely new country. We had just gotten off a climate-controlled, boring, sad sort of plane, and Cambodia was humid, hot, and full of life. There were Christmas lights on the trees, houses in bright colors, and it was night-time, so the sounds and smells stood out more. We rode to our hotel in tuk-tuks, which are colorful open-air carts pulled by noisy motorcycles. The traffic was hectic, the voices were speaking a language I didn't understand, plus I was deliriously tired from twenty-four hours on a plane during which I neither slept nor ate. All in all it was a wonderful, dizzying moment.

Q: How did you share your experiences with others once you returned?

A: That was the most difficult part of the trip. When

people asked me how the trip went, they didn't want a long dialogue about how amazing and fantastic it was; they wanted a short summation. The most common question was "What was your favorite part?" I didn't have a favorite part. The whole trip was so eye-opening! I told most people that my favorite part was visiting the school, because that was an easy answer.

Q: What's it like to ride an elephant?

A: You have to climb a fire escape–like structure to get on its back. At first, the swaying of the elephant makes you feel like you're going to fall off, and it's weird that everyone is staring at you. One little boy pointed at us and said, "Oh my!" But after I got over the initial shock, it was really enjoyable.

Q: Did this trip turn you into a lifelong traveler?

A: Definitely. I can't wait to go somewhere else. Once you see that the world is much bigger than you thought, your perspective will never shrink back to its old size.

THE INNOVATORS AND RISK-TAKERS
You Gotta Meet an Entrepreneur!

There are lots of good ideas out there that will make money. In fact, most of us have had at least one cool new business idea where we say, "If someone made (or did) that, they'd make a fortune!" A person who takes the risks of starting a new business and doesn't listen to the voices all around that may say "this is a bad idea" and "you're going to fail" is an entrepreneur.

Known as passionate, forward-thinking risk takers, entrepreneurs turn great ideas into even better businesses—building foundations for selling their ideas and making money for themselves and for their employees and investors. We need entrepreneurs for growth, new jobs, and the fresh ideas that keep our communities vibrant. Meeting one (or more!) will help you take your great ideas to the next level.

Strategies

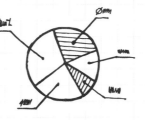

- Ask family, friends, and teachers for local companies in your community. Look up these companies' stories online and see if the entrepreneur who started the business is still there. Ask him or her for an interview.
- If you have a good idea for a business, ask the entrepreneurs that you have found for advice

on starting up and becoming an entrepreneur yourself.

- Look into entrepreneurship programs for kids that pair up students with successful business leaders. If there is no such program where you live, start one! It can be your very first business venture.

Ask Away

- What did you need in order to start your business?
- Did you have a lot of supporters or did most people think you were crazy to start your own business?
- What's your best advice for kids who want to be entrepreneurs?
- What would you do differently if you were just starting your business today?

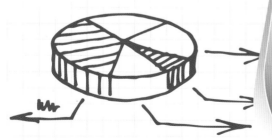

SOME FAMOUS ENTREPRENEURS

MAYA PENN
GARY GOLDBERG
STEVE JOBS
DEBBI FIELDS

Check It Out

A website about and for young entrepreneurs: *www.youngentrepreneur.com*
Tips for kids and teens who want to start their own businesses: *bit.ly/RIktmR*
Meet some young entrepreneurs: *onforb.es/mUHImu*

"All achievements, all earned riches, have their beginning in an idea." —Napoleon Hill

I'D LIKE TO INTRODUCE YOU TO MAYA PENN

Maya Shea Penn is a thirteen-year-old entrepreneur, philanthropist, designer, artist, animator, illustrator, and writer who lives in Atlanta, Georgia. She is the CEO of Maya's Ideas (*www.mayasideas.com*), a company she started in 2008 when she was just eight years old. She creates handmade, one-of-a-kind, eco-friendly accessories and clothing. She has been featured in several newspapers, websites, and magazines and has customers in the United States, Denmark, Italy, Australia, and more.

Q: How did you get interested in becoming an entrepreneur?

A: To be honest, I started my business out of curiosity. At first I started making little headbands out of ribbon for myself to wear. When I wore them, people would stop me and say, "Hey, that's a really cute headband! Where can I buy one?" So I thought, *Wow, I can start my own business!*

Q: How does your community help you and how do you help your community?

A: I knew two things when I started my business. One, all of my items had to be eco-friendly and I had to use materials that didn't harm the environment; and two, up to 20 percent of the profits I made would go to local and global charities and environmental organizations. My community helps me by being awesome supporters!

Q: What did you need to get your business off the ground?

A: I had to learn a lot about my business, like branding and marketing, social media, and learning about my audience and my customers, and seeing what items sold the most and what items sold the least, and listening to the feedback of my customers.

Q: Did you have a lot of supporters or did most people think you were crazy?

A: Well, people didn't think I was crazy, but some didn't know I would be so successful this young.

Q: What's your best advice for kids who want to be entrepreneurs?

A: The advice I have for other kid entrepreneurs is, it's important to know what your ideas are. Start an idea book, a journal where you can write down all of your ideas for your business. Whether it be a small thought that crosses your mind or the next big idea, it's important to have it written down. Even if it doesn't seem important, it may be very useful in the future. You also have to research what you want to do and what field of business you want to be in. Most importantly, you have to believe in yourself and what you're doing. When people know that you have a passion and you truly want to achieve something, you'll be amazed at how much support you will get. Don't get discouraged if things are going slower than you expected. If things seem to be going wrong, don't give up too quickly. It's good for things to go wrong in a business, because it's a learning experience and it helps you and your business grow.

Q: What are your plans for the future?

A: Many times people ask me what I want to do in five years or more. I see myself doing exactly what I'm doing now: being an entrepreneur, philanthropist, and animated filmmaker, and doing everything I can to help the planet. I may be one person, but the smallest actions can lead to the biggest changes. That's why everyone should get involved with saving our environment and giving back to our communities through doing what you love. :)

HaVE aNY GOOD iDEaS LaTELY?

SHOWING US WHAT THEY SEE
You Gotta Meet an Artist!

You've probably seen all sorts of famous paintings and drawings by artists such as Leonardo da Vinci, Vincent van Gogh, Pablo Picasso, Andy Warhol, and more. They've been gone for a long time, although their work remains in museums all over the world. You can't meet these guys, but there are artists everywhere in our communities. They teach at your school and at nearby colleges, and they show their work at local community centers, museums, and galleries. And many of them would love to meet you!

Strategies

- Ask your school's art teacher if he or she is an artist. Do they paint, draw, sculpt? Then ask if they have any shows (where they present their work) coming up.
- If your teacher doesn't have anything to share with you, ask if there are any local art show openings you can attend. An opening is the first day an artist's work is shown at a gallery. It's usually a party with

food and beverages, and the artist or artists who have works in the show are there to meet with people and answer questions. Sometimes you need an invitation, but other times anyone can attend. Once you arrive at the opening, look for a crowd of people standing around someone speaking. This could very well be one of the artists. Before approaching the artist, take a look at their work. Spend some time getting to know their style and get a sense of how you feel about it. Then introduce yourself, tell them what you think of their work, and see how long you can keep the conversation going. If they're really busy at the event, ask if they would be interested in coming to your school for a visit or if you could interview them.

SOME FAMOUS ARTISTS

MARY CASSATT
EDWARD HOPPER
ANTONY GORMLEY
MARJETICA POTRC

- Sign up for weekend art classes to meet teachers and other students who are artists.

- Go into an art gallery and ask the curator if any of the work they are showcasing is from local artists. Then ask if they'll be coming to the gallery at all. You can even ask the curator if he would pass your contact information to the artist. If the artist can't meet with you, they may be willing to e-mail with you.

- Check newspapers and community boards for studio tours. Some artists will occasionally open to the public the studios where they work.

Ask Away

- Where do you get the ideas for your work?
- Why did you want to become an artist?
- How can I become an artist?
- How do you get your artwork into a museum or gallery?
- What media (like paint, pencil, or digital) do you like to work in?
- How did you practice your art when you were a kid?
- What's your favorite person, place, or thing to draw, sculpt, paint, etc.?

Check It Out

The Museum of Modern Art: www.moma.org

The National Gallery of Art's kid page: www.nga.gov/kids

Gallery of famous artists: www.famousartistsgallery.com

FUN Fact

THE YOUNGEST INTERNATIONALLY RECOGNIZED PAINTER IN THE WORLD IS SIX-YEAR-OLD AELITA ANDRE. AELITA LIVES IN AUSTRALIA AND HAS BEEN PAINTING SINCE SHE WAS TWO. HER WORK HAS SOLD FOR THOUSANDS OF DOLLARS, AND HER SHOWS REGULARLY SELL OUT. CHECK HER OUT AT WWW.AELITAANDRE.COM.

"The purpose of art is washing the dust of daily life off our souls." —Pablo Picasso

ORDER IN THE COURT
You Gotta Meet a Judge!

Flip the TV channels during the day and sooner or later you'll come across a man or woman wearing a black robe, looking down on two people standing across from each other. These people will be arguing about something—money, a pet, a lawn mower—and the person in the robe is asking questions, trying to figure out who was wrong in this matter and who was right. This person is a judge. Although these TV judges will often be yelling and dispensing advice, a real judge's job is quite different.

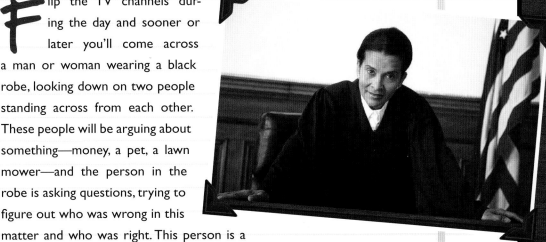

Judges preside over court proceedings all over the country. That means they are in charge of the courtroom and what goes on inside it. They are impartial, meaning they don't take sides, and as they listen to witnesses and look at evidence, they often have to interpret and apply laws to decide whether someone is guilty of breaking the law. Sometimes there are juries that decide verdicts (guilt or innocence), but other times the judge is in charge of making the decision. Depending on where you live, you may have federal or district judges living nearby, but most likely the judges you'll come into contact with are state judges.

Strategies

- About half of the states in the United States elect their judges, and a good time to meet a judge is when he or she is up for election. Look for functions where they may be and see if you can get their attention after a speech.

- Sit in on courtroom proceedings that are open to the public.
- Write to a judge's office asking for a class visit or for a personal meeting.
- When meeting a judge in a courthouse, or even if you're just visiting a courtroom, make sure to dress up, and don't wear a hat! Most judges are called "Your Honor."

Ask Away

- Why do judges wear black robes? What do you wear under yours?
- Can you describe a really difficult decision you once had to make?
- Were you elected or appointed? Which do you think is the best way to choose judges?
- What's the best way to meet a judge?
- What's a mistrial?

SOME FAMOUS JUDGES

THURGOOD MARSHALL
JOHN G. ROBERTS
SONIA SOTOMAYOR
JUDGE JUDY (JUDITH SHEINDLIN)

The Supreme Court of the United States

Check It Out

Los Angeles's judge community outreach program:

www.lasuperiorcourt.org/outreach/ui

Courtroom in the Classroom Program:

www.ninth.courts.state.oh.us/school.htm

Information on how our courts work:

people.howstuffworks.com/judicial-system.htm

"The right to swing my fist ends where the other man's nose begins." —Oliver Wendell Holmes

 # THE COURTROOM iN THE CLaSSROOM PROGRaM

The Courtroom in the Classroom Program is an educational outreach program in Ohio that provides high school students with experience in how the judicial system works. Judges travel to schools to hear two or three actual oral arguments involving real cases pending before the court. The court generally chooses to hear interesting cases that will grab the students' attention and provide great material for students and teachers to discuss after judges leave.

The court may schedule a question-and-answer session with the participating lawyers after the oral arguments, and sometimes students meet in small groups with the judges. In two recent outings, judges had lunch with a group of students who were able to talk to them about a variety of topics, from how they became judges to why they wear robes.

The Courtroom in the Classroom Program provides a unique learning opportunity for students, teachers, and judges, and it brings the judicial process to students who might otherwise never witness it in action. If you're interested in organizing a program like this, get a teacher or parent to help you petition the courthouse near you.

GIVING BACK
You Gotta Meet a Volunteer!

C ommunities can only thrive when their members pitch in and help, and most of this help comes from people who volunteer their free time without getting paid. These volunteers work at animal rescue centers, food distribution warehouses, homeless shelters, soup kitchens, disaster relief centers, retirement homes, and more. Most are very busy people who nonetheless believe that they can do something to make a difference in someone else's life, and they're happy to do it. Volunteers come in all shapes, sizes, and ages, and you can meet one just about anywhere you turn—at school, church, scout meetings, and local events, to name a few.

Strategies

• The best way to meet a volunteer is to become one yourself! For example, if you're interested in the environment, volunteer at a local recycling center. You're bound to meet other like-minded environmentalists who get excited about the same things you do. Worried about an elderly neighbor who just moved into a retirement

home? Organize a school trip to the home and pair up with elderly buddies. You can read with them, share your artwork or a recital piece you've been working on, or just listen to their stories.

- Ask about volunteer opportunities at your church, synagogue, or mosque, or any organization you belong to.
- Join the Boy or Girl Scouts or other service-oriented organizations.
- Ask a teacher or school counselor for ideas of how to meet and/or become a volunteer.
- You may feel uncomfortable helping out folks who are less fortunate than you, and that's perfectly okay. Anytime you leave the comfort zone of your life for a new, challenging experience, you're bound to feel a little strange. One way to help with this is to ask family members, friends, or teachers if they might be willing to go with you until you feel more comfortable on your own.

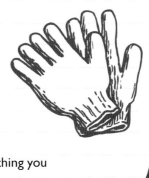

SOME FAMOUS VOLUNTEERS

JIMMY CARTER
SALLY RIDE
PRINCESS DIANA
MATT DAMON

Ask Away

- Why do you volunteer?
- How does it make you feel?
- Do you feel like you're making a difference? How?
- What's your best advice for getting involved in something you care about?

35

Check It Out

Information on becoming a volunteer: *bit.ly/gLM3JP*

More information on becoming a volunteer: *bit.ly/9Nuphr*

Getting the whole family involved: *www.doinggoodtogether.org*

Resources and stories about volunteering: *www.volunteerweekly.org*

"When you're a kid, you can easily feel like you have nothing to give: no money to donate, no knowledge to share. But kids do have time and energy (we hope). And that is all that it takes to lend a hand."—Katie Robinson

Food Donations

Habitat for Humanity®

Habitat for Humanity is a nonprofit Christian ministry "founded on the conviction that every man, woman, and child should have a decent, safe, and affordable place to live." They build affordable houses for low-income families around the world, and they are always in need of volunteers. Youth United is an affiliated program in which community youth come together to completely fund and build a Habitat home. Youth ages five to twenty-five serve as the leaders, planners, fund-raisers, and public relations specialists, while youth ages sixteen to twenty-five build the house on site. For more information, visit www.habitatyouthprograms.org/youthunited.

MEET MY FRIEND KATIE ROBINSON—SHE'S a VOLUNTEER

Katie Robinson lives in Baltimore, Maryland, with her husband. She spends her days working at her own company, BW Kids Consulting, which helps families work out their problems. She also takes time out of her busy schedule to volunteer, something she's been doing since she was a kid. Here's what she has to say about it:

"I wouldn't say that my upbringing was overwhelmed with volunteering and service opportunities. I wouldn't say that every weekend I was out doing something for the good of others. But somehow, almost unbeknownst to me, I learned some lessons from the volunteer experiences of my youth. It's only when I take a moment to reflect that I even realize that my early experiences have shaped me into a real-life volunteer. Who knew?

"Girl Scouts and church: These were the two places where I first got my feet wet in the volunteer world. I began by raising money for and participating in the Crop Walk, a whopping six-mile walk that my little legs definitely felt by the end. Easy. Once a year. And back in the days of no inhibitions, when asking neighbors for a little money was no big deal. Success!

"From then, I went on to Christmas caroling at area nursing homes, helping to hand out food at the food bank, sending care packages to soldiers in the Gulf, and putting on puppet shows at a local church for underserved kids. These activities didn't happen all the time, but once you do a little volunteering, it helps to pave the way for more. I didn't even always want to do them, but the expectation was there, so I kept on trucking.

"By the time I reached college, I guess my course was fixed. I did what plenty of other college kids do (eat too much, sleep too much, not study enough), but I also returned to the idea of helping others and became a volunteer again. I spent a spring break in Guatemala building cinder block houses. I coordinated with other volunteers to create a weekly violence prevention program that took place in a Washington, DC, public school classroom. I have read with kids, tutored kids, sorted food, taught parenting classes. The list of 'time-giving' goes on. I say this not to be self-righteous or pious in my volunteerism, but because I never really considered how the backdrop of helping out in my younger life has really created my apparent continued commitment to volunteering. At least not until I wrote this.

"I even 'volunteer' by singing in a community choir. Though I'm not 'helping' anyone or scoring brownie points for myself, I am still giving something: my effort and my time. That's all volunteering is, no?"

ALL THE WORLD'S A STAGE
You Gotta Meet an Actor!

When it comes to celebrities, we tend to adore and/or despise actors the most. They make lots of money and look glamorous doing it. Whole magazines and websites are devoted to following these celebs around and reporting on their smallest moves and misdeeds. Most of us won't meet too many of these superstars, but every community has actors who are either trying to make it big or are happy acting in plays in and around town. Some are amateurs who act because it's fun to pretend to be someone else or because they get a sense of joy performing in front of an audience. Others work at their craft because they want to act for a living.

Strategies

HOLLYWOOD

- Look for ways you can volunteer your time at a local stage company or theater. You may be able to help paint sets, work on costumes, or even man the lights.
- Audition for plays that are looking for kids or that need singers for a chorus. You may only have a small part, but you'll spend a lot of time with actors who would love to talk to you.
- Take classes offered by theaters. They are usually taught by actors.
- Go to plays and introduce yourself to the actors after the performance. Ask for a follow-up meeting or an interview.

SOME FAMOUS ACTORS

EMMA WATSON
JOHNNY DEPP
JENNIFER LAWRENCE
DONALD GLOVER

Ask Away

- Why do you act?
- What was your favorite part you've ever played?
- What part do you wish you could play?
- What sort of acting training do you have?
- Do you wish you were a movie star?
- How can a kid get into acting?

Check It Out

Resources and information on acting: www.theactorslife.com/craft/index.html

A nationwide community theater directory: bit.ly/12jQsnb

A nonprofit organization dedicated to discovering and developing independent artists in film: www.sundance.org

"With any part you play, there is a certain amount of yourself in it. There has to be, otherwise it's just not acting. It's lying."—Johnny Depp

41

YEARNING TO BREATHE FREE
You Gotta Meet an Immigrant!

Unless your ancestors were American Indians, you come from immigrants. That means at some point, your family once called another country home, then came to the United States to live. Maybe they were looking for freedoms that didn't exist in their country. Perhaps they were looking for better jobs, a different life, or a brighter future.

The United States is often referred to as a melting pot—a place where countless cultures mix and blend, creating something new. That's because so much of our population is made up of immigrants! It can also be thought of as a stew or a salad, with each ingredient in the recipe keeping its own flavor (culture). Whether your family has been in this country for one year or three hundred years, introduce yourself to an immigrant and continue the long tradition of cultures coming together and learning about each other so they can live together peacefully as friends and neighbors.

Strategies

- Talk to classmates, teammates, or fellow club members that you know are from other countries or have parents or grandparents from other countries. Ask them about their experiences here and in their homeland.
- Ask one of your teachers if you can do a class project celebrating diversity in the classroom.
- Volunteer at an organization that helps recent immigrants in your hometown.

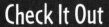

Ask Away

- What is your home country like?
- What made you decide to leave?
- What do you like about where we live? What do you dislike?
- How difficult was it to get here?
- What do you most miss about your home country?
- What do you think of the United States' immigration laws?
- Do you feel like an American?

Check It Out

Take a virtual tour of Ellis Island: *bit.ly/csdYxR*
Profiles of young immigrants: *bit.ly/Kq4eck*
Immigration facts for kids: *to.pbs.org/XSIfVx*

Between 1886 and 1924, nearly 14 million immigrants entered the U.S. through New York, and one of the first things they saw was the Statue of Liberty.

"Recognize yourself in he and she who are not like you and me."—Carlos Fuentes

Ryan Bastin (center) lives in the United States, but both his parents are from the southern hemisphere. Monica, his mom, was born in Peru, while his dad, Mark, is from Canberra, Australia. If you meet this international family, ask them to cook you up some seviche, Papa a la Huancaína, or alfajores.

SOME FAMOUS IMMIGRANTS

ALBERT EINSTEIN
ROBINSON CANO
KHALED HOSSEINI
CHARLIZE THERON

43

THE MENU MAKERS
You Gotta Meet a Chef!

If you're the kind of kid who offers to cook dinner every night, or if you like to whip up fancy desserts for your family, then you should definitely meet a chef. A chef's job is to manage a restaurant or bakery's kitchen. That means they develop the menu, find the right foods for the recipes, hire and manage the cooks, and prepare and cook the meals. Some chefs collect all their favorite recipes and write cookbooks, while others become teachers or even appear on television or radio to share their love of food.

Strategies

- The next time you're at your favorite restaurant, ask the waiter if you can meet the chef or tour the kitchen. The chef will probably be too busy to spend a lot of time with you right then; however, see if you can plan a time for a more thorough visit—perhaps just before the kitchen gears up for the day.
- Look for weekend cooking classes that let kids participate.

Ask Away

- How did you learn to be a chef?
- What's your favorite recipe?
- Do you ever just throw stuff together without a recipe?
- Why do chefs have big white hats?

SOME FAMOUS CHEFS

Julia Child
Gordon Ramsay
Emeril Lagasse
Rachael Ray

44

Check It Out

A cooking school for kids: www.youngchefsacademy.com

Read about some famous chefs:

www.biography.com/people/groups/chefs

A word or two from the White House assistant chef:

1.usa.gov/HEqIG4

"No one is born a great cook. One learns by doing."—Julia Child

GETTING THE WORDS RIGHT
You Gotta Meet a Writer!

Words, words, everywhere! They're in books, sprawled across your computer screen, and on your cereal boxes, and writers are the ones who put those words together to tell a story, teach you something, entertain you, or even sell you something. You probably have a favorite famous author, and he or she is probably very, very busy. But there are writers all around you! They may have other jobs in addition to writing, or if they're lucky, they can support themselves solely through their craft. And many would love to meet you.

Strategies

- Ask a local bookstore if they have any local author book signings planned.
- Ask your school librarian if he or she knows any authors personally.
- With your teacher's permission, ask an author to visit your classroom.
- Many authors (especially those who write books for kids) tour schools and bookstores promoting books or teaching. Ask your school if they have a budget for bringing in authors, and then see if they'll invite a local author to come.
- Look up authors online and write to them if they give you the opportunity on their websites.

Make sure you've read something by the author before contacting him or her.

• Offer to interview the author for the school newspaper.

Ask Away

• How do you deal with writer's block?
• What advice do you give to new writers?
• Do you keep a journal? Why or why not?
• Where do you get your ideas?
• Can you tell me a little about your writing process?
• What are some of your favorite books?

Check It Out

Writing tools and club for kids: *www.kidwritersclub.com* and *www.kidpub.com*

Discover a new favorite author: *bit.ly/12m2Yie*

SOME FAMOUS WRITERS

J. K. ROWLING
ROALD DAHL
JUDY BLUME
EOIN COLFER

"Writing—the art of communicating thoughts to the mind, through the eye—is the great invention of the world."—Abraham Lincoln

INTRODUCING KELLY MILNER HALLS, WRITER EXTRAORDINAIRE

Mysterious mummies! Bigfoot! Dinosaurs! Wild dogs! Ghosts! Aliens! If you ever meet Kelly Milner Halls, she can tell you about these things and more, because she has written about all of them. Kelly is the author of more than thirty books for kids, and if you live in the Pacific Northwest (she lives in Spokane, Washington), you may have a chance to meet her, because when she's not writing, she's visiting schools, often bringing along a few of the fossils in her collection.

Q: **How many schools do you visit a year?**

A: I visit between forty and sixty schools each year, and I love every one. School visits keep me connected to the kids who read my books.

Q: **Which of your books is your favorite and why?**

A: *Tales of the Cryptids* seems to be the favorite among kids, so that makes it my favorite, too. But I love all of my books. If I didn't, I wouldn't have written them.

Q: **What's the best way to meet you?**

A: I've had people call the school I'm visiting and ask if they can attend, even if they aren't students. That's always fun. And I've had people ask if they can take me to dinner while I'm in their hometown to talk about writing or books. That's fine, too. I try to say yes whenever I can. I remember being a beginner, and I do my best to help however I can.

Q: **What's your advice for getting a writer to come to a school?**

A: The best way to get an author to visit is to ask. They have a set fee most of the time, but if you can't afford that fee, tell them what you can afford, if anything. We really do try to be flexible—many of us. So ask and give us the opportunity to work with you. *Yes* is always more fun than *no*.

Q: **How does your neighborhood or community support you as a writer?**

A: There is a great SCBWI (Society of Children's Book Writers and Illustrators) in Spokane that a writer named Kenn Nesbitt and I started many years ago. Other people keep it going now, but it's grown to be a really fine resource for children's writers and illustrators in Spokane and Northern Idaho. They are very supportive, but so are my local elementary schools. They have embraced me and my work, and I do all I can to help them, too. It takes a village, and together, we've created a very nice place to inspire young people to dream and work toward their dreams. It's all about *you*, the kids!

LEADERS AND LEGISLATORS
You Gotta Meet a Politician!

The president of the United States lives in the White House and has Secret Service agents all around him. You can write to him, and if you're lucky, you may get a form letter back. Same goes for U.S. congressmen. But there are politicians making important decisions in your community, and it's a lot easier to meet them.

Depending on how close you live to your state's capital, you may be able to meet your governor or a state senator. If you live in a smaller city, you may be able to meet the mayor or city/county council members. These politicians make important decisions and cast decisive votes on issues regarding your schools, how and where businesses can operate in your town, how much to pay police officers and firefighters, and much, much more. Whether or not you have an issue you'd like to see solved with a politician's help, getting to know who represents you and your community is always a good idea. Not only does it keep you up-to-date on what's going on around you, but it lets the leaders know that you and others are paying attention.

 Terry Bellamy, the mayor of this author's hometown!

SOME FAMOUS POLITICIANS

BARACK OBAMA
HILLARY CLINTON
GEORGE W. BUSH
ABRAHAM LINCOLN

Strategies

- Many local politicians have other jobs and only perform their civic duties part-time. Find out when they're available and make an appointment to meet then.
- A great time to meet politicians is when they're up for election. Politicians need lots of help getting elected. By helping them, you could get to watch the politician give speeches, shake hands, and debate policy with those he or she is running against.
- Suggest a school visit to a local politician.

Ask Away

- What drove you to become a politician?
- Do you like running for office? Why or why not?
- What's the most difficult part of your job?
- Do you want to be president someday? Why or why not?
- What issues do you believe shouldn't be solved by politicians?

Check It Out

The official kids' site of the U.S. government:
kids.usa.gov/government/index.shtml

A directory of great government sites for kids: *bit.ly/14HelQi*

Learn about the branches of government and more: *www.congressforkids.net*

"Change will not come if we wait for some other person or if we wait for some other time. We are the ones we've been waiting for. We are the change we seek."
—Barack Obama

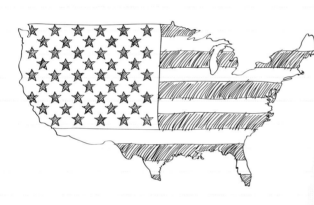

Up until the early 1900s, job seekers and those looking for favors could wait in line to meet with the president—a tradition Abraham Lincoln disliked greatly because it kept him from getting any work done.

WITH FAITH AND UNDERSTANDING
You Gotta Meet Someone from a Different Religion!

Whether or not you and your family practice a particular religion, it's good to meet someone who worships differently from you. It could be a friend, a teacher, or a neighbor, and even if a different religion might seem alien to you, it'll be cool to see how it differs from yours and how it is similar.

Communities are made up of lots of different people who believe different things about God, what happens when we die, why we're here on Earth, and other big questions. Comparing and finding common ground can go a long way toward breaking down the walls that keep people apart from one another—finding friendship where there was once only fear and distrust.

Strategies

• If you already know of someone in your community who practices a different religion, try meeting them where they worship. Take some time to learn the basics of how they worship so that when you arrive you won't feel quite so uncomfortable.

• Look up local places of worship online or in the phone book. (Christians worship in churches and their leaders are priests or pastors. Muslims worship in mosques, and their leaders are imams or mullahs. Jews worship in synagogues and their leaders are called rabbis. Hindus worship in temples and their spiritual leaders are called priests.) Call and ask for the hours they are open and, stating your purpose, ask if you can meet one of the place's leaders.

- Ask a friend or classmate who worships a different religion if you can go with them when they worship. Learn as much as possible and write down your questions, which you can ask your friend, his family, or the religion's leader.

Ask Away

- How is your religion different from mine?
- What are your religion's main beliefs?
- What questions do you have about my religion?
- Do you face discrimination about your beliefs?

SOME FAMOUS
RELIGIOUS
LEADERS

MARTIN LUTHER KING, JR.
THE Dalai Lama
MAHATMA GANDHI
ST. FRANCIS OF ASSISI

Check It Out

Explore the world's major religions: *bit.ly/ZHE2hj* and *www.uri.org/kids/world.htm* and *www.bbc.co.uk/religion/religions*

"Just as a candle cannot burn without fire, humans cannot live without a spiritual life."
—Buddha

TO SERVE AND PROTECT
You Gotta Meet a Police Officer!

Communities would have a hard time existing without rules and laws, as well as without the people in charge of making sure these rules and laws are being followed—police officers. In your community, the police keep the peace by enforcing laws, protecting you and your property, and investigating crimes. They arrest those who have broken the law and make sure that justice is served.

Being a police officer can be a risky and stressful job, and officers often work long hours and night shifts. It's not a great time to introduce yourself to police officers while they're busy working (pulling your mom over for speeding, for instance); however, try saying hi to an officer walking their beat (patrolling) and see if they have a minute for a chat.

Strategies

- Some schools are assigned police officers who patrol the hallways, direct traffic, provide student counseling and education, and make sure students are following the rules of the school as well as the laws of the community. They are called school resource officers (SROs). Introduce yourself to your school's SRO and ask to do an interview.
- Plan a visit to the local police department. Many offer school visits that include getting fingerprints and spending a couple minutes in lockup (as long as nobody's already in there).

Ask Away

- What are some of the things you do to help the community?
- What do you like most/least about your job?
- Why did you decide to become a police officer?
- What sort of equipment do you have to carry with you?
- How much paperwork do you have to fill out for each incident you investigate?

Check It Out

What it's like to be a police officer: www.bls.gov/k12/law01.htm and bit.ly/14HiMA7

A police officer's resource page: www.policeone.com

"My heroes are those who risk their lives every day to protect our world and make it a better place—police, firefighters, and members of our armed forces." —Sidney Sheldon

SOME FAMOUS POLICE OFFICERS

FRANK SERPICO
TEDDY ROOSEVELT
DANIEL BOONE
JENNIFER FULFORD-SALVANO

WHAT YOU WILL FIND ON A POLICE OFFICER'S BELT

Police officers carry up to twenty pounds of equipment with them while out on patrol. This can include:

- gun
- gun holster
- pepper or other chemical spray
- handcuffs
- radio
- flashlight/keys
- baton (nightstick)
- first-aid kit
- disposable gloves
- bullets
- notebook/pen
- ECD (electronic control device, such as a Taser)

GOING THE EXTRA MILE
You Gotta Meet an Athlete!

When you watch a pro athlete run, kick or throw a ball, or jump and flip in the air, it can be like watching the impossible. It's one of the reasons these athletes are so revered in our culture. We treat them like superstars and want them to be role models. But behind each highlight video are thousands of hours of practicing and training, coaches and parents teaching and motivating, and the will of a person failing and failing … until he or she succeeds. Each community has athletes who are doing what it takes to make it, and if you want to see this sort of determination and hard work before it pays off, find an athlete in your hometown.

Strategies

- Many community coaches were once athletes. Find out by asking your coach if you're on a sports team.

- Find out if your hometown hosts a developmental league or a minor league baseball team. You can get a lot closer to the action at these games, and you'll meet some of tomorrow's stars before they make it big. Get autographs, ask for interviews, root for these athletes, and wish them luck!
- Attend high school sporting events and talk to a coach after the game. See if they would be open to asking team members if they'd like to be interviewed.
- Offer to write profiles for your school newspaper or for a blog.
- If the Olympics are coming up, ask around to see if there are any local athletes attempting to make the team. Interview them.

Ask Away

- How many times a week do you practice?
- Where do you see yourself in five years?
- Do you plan on making sports your career? Why or why not?
- Who do you admire most as an athlete? Why?

Check It Out

Muhammad Ali's website: *www.ali.com*

The U.S. Olympics website: *www.teamusa.org*

Minor League Baseball: *www.milb.com/index.jsp*

The NBA's development league: *www.nba.us/dleague*

"I wish people would love everybody else the way they love me. It would be a better world."—Muhammad Ali

SOME FAMOUS ATHLETES

TIM DUNCAN

ALEX MORGAN

MUHAMMAD ALI

LISA LESLIE

THE DREAMERS OF DREAMS
You Gotta Meet a Musician!

Music has been a part of human societies for thousands of years, and scientists have proven that music affects our brains, releasing chemicals that make us happy. No wonder we love our musicians—the people who combine sound, melody, harmony, and rhythm into noise patterns that thrill us. The musicians in your neighborhood play in parks, restaurants, talent shows, battles of the bands, parties, and other places. Whether you play an instrument or you just love listening, become a fan and make a point of meeting the band.

Strategies

- Attend local shows at venues such as restaurants, clubs, and theaters. Stay behind after the show and start asking questions. It helps if you're familiar with their music and you can talk about other musicians who play a similar style.
- Ask your school if they'll support a lunchtime concert series. Help the school identify local musicians to contact and see if they'd be open to performing short sets during lunch.

Ask Away

- How did you get interested in music?
- How did you end up playing the instrument you play now?
- What's the best way for a kid to start a band?
- How old were you when you first played in front of an audience?
- Which bands and musicians do you recommend kids listen to?

SOME FAMOUS MUSICIANS

AARON COPLAND
JOHN COLTRANE
TAYLOR SWIFT
BILLY JOEL

Check It Out

An organization that brings bands to schools: www.musicmakesmusic.org

A great place to discover emerging musicians: www.independentmusicawards.com/ima

"I think music in itself is healing. It's an explosive expression of humanity. It's something we are all touched by. No matter what culture we're from, everyone loves music." —Billy Joel

TO THE RESCUE!
You Gotta Meet an Animal Rescuer!

According to the Humane Society of the United States, the nation's largest animal protection agency, approximately six to eight million dogs and cats are sent to local animal shelters. These animals have either been abandoned by their owners, found wandering the streets, or have otherwise become homeless. Animal rescue workers and volunteers work to decrease this number and find homes for these pets. Rescue workers at the shelters keep the animals healthy until their owners or new homes are found, and they actively seek new owners to adopt a pet from a shelter rather than buy one. To make sure animals don't reproduce, which can leave communities with even more homeless animals, animal rescue workers also sponsor spay and neuter clinics.

Strategies

- Volunteer at a local animal shelter and get to know the folks who spend so much of their time helping these wonderful animals.
- Talk to neighbors about how they got their pets. If they rescued them, ask about the process and the group the pets were rescued from.
- Consider adopting a pet of your own through an animal shelter.

Ask Away

• Why do you work as an animal rescuer?

• What's your view on euthanizing animals who can't find a home?

• How many pets do you have?

• Is this your full-time job or are you a volunteer?

Check It Out

The first humane organization: www.aspca.org

Website for the TV show *Animal Rescue*: www.animalrescuetv.com

A national no-kill shelter for animals: www.bestfriends.org

The Humane Society's animal shelter page: animalsheltering.org

"Whoever said 'Money can't buy happiness' never paid an adoption fee."—popular animal shelter slogan

SOME FAMOUS RESCUERS

Dian Fossey
Cesar Millan
Betty White
Russell Simmons

ASK ME ANYTHING
You Gotta Meet a Librarian!

Surely you know what a librarian is, and you've more than likely talked to one before—especially if you needed help finding a book or article for a school assignment. Librarians serve the community by knowing *a lot* about finding information. If you need a question answered and your librarian doesn't know the answer, he or she will be able to tell you where to go to find it—whether it's in a book, magazine, newspaper, or website. But what are librarians like when they're not behind the desk? Why don't you find out?

Strategies

- This one is easy—go to a library and introduce yourself to the man or woman behind the desk. Ask them if they're open to an interview or just start asking questions.
- One way to get a librarian talking is to talk about favorite books and authors. Ask what their

suggestions are and offer some of your own.
- Many libraries need volunteers to help shelve books and more. Spend some time helping out and you'll get to know the staff quickly.

Ask Away

- How do you know so much about things?
- What are some of your favorite hobbies?
- How have computers changed your job?

SOME FAMOUS LIBRARIANS

BEN FRANKLIN
MELVIL DEWEY
BEVERLY CLEARY
LAURA BUSH

Check It Out!

Book lover and famous librarian: www.nancypearl.com
Library history: www.libraryhistorybuff.com/benfranklin.htm

"I have always imagined that paradise will be a kind of library."—Jorge Luis Borges

Benjamin Franklin's personal library had more than four thousand volumes, and he set up the nation's first public library, called the Library Company of Philadelphia.

MEET MY FRIEND JENNIFER COLEMAN, a LIBRARIAN

Jennifer is a librarian at an elementary school in a suburban school district north of Austin, Texas, that used to be farmland but is now becoming a bustling, family-centered city. She serves nine hundred students from kindergarten through fifth grade and about one hundred faculty and staff. Jennifer considers her role in the community to be putting books in the hands of children and teaching them how to use information.

Q: What's your favorite book and why?

A: Librarians typically answer this by saying, "That is like trying to choose your favorite child! It can't be done." And this is so true! I have been a librarian since 1996, and over the years, books on the shelves are not just books on the shelves—they become personified to me in many ways.

For instance, I was chosen to attend a special conference in New York where my mentors were giants in the book world, like two-time Newbery winner Jerry Spinelli. I had just finished reading his novel *Milkweed*, and there were some specific scenes that were gut-wrenching and seared in my thoughts. Over the course of the conference, I was able to have some conversations with Mr. Spinelli about those specific scenes, and it deepened my connection to the book. Whenever I see someone by the *F SPI* section of the library, I can't help but book-talk a Spinelli title, because I know they are in for a treat by an author who deeply cares and who is a craftsman with words.

Other books I feel the same way about include *A Long Way from Chicago* by Richard Peck, *The Whingdingdilly* by Bill Peet (the first book I ever remember checking out when I was a first grader), Beverly Cleary's books, *Charlie and the Chocolate Factory* by Roald Dahl, *Tales of a Fourth Grade Nothing* by Judy Blume (because I get nostalgic for my childhood), and *Dead End in Norvelt* by Jack Gantos! But it is hard to pick a favorite one. I guess overall, I love books that stick.

Q: What is the most common question you get at the library?

A: "Where's a good book?" Sometimes there are so many choices, kids (and teachers!) get overwhelmed. They tend to get the same books over and over because it's easy. That's why that kindergartner keeps asking me for *Pinkalicious* even though there are only four of them and we have sixteen thousand other titles. I try to teach people to have a lot of strategies so they can answer the question for themselves:

- Read the blurbs on the backs.
- See an interesting cover? Open up the book and give it a chance!
- Look at displays. (We librarians put a lot of time and thought into those!)
- Look at the return cart for the "frequent fliers."
- Ask a friend, "What's the last good book you read?"
- Ask an adult you love, "Tell me something you read when you were my age."

- Ask a librarian. We're full of good ideas!
- Ask your teacher.
- Be nice to the bottom shelves . . . sometimes we need to look in places we don't usually look!

Q: What's the best part about your job?

A: It was 1999, and I was book-talking the Newbery Award–winner *Holes* by Louis Sachar, which I was crazy about. I basically poured every ounce of enthusiasm I had into this book talk to a group of fourth graders, and before you knew it, every fourth grader in our school had a personal copy. I thought, *Wow, mission accomplished!* But it didn't end there. Four years later, during the holidays—the time of year our school often received visits from students who were alumni—I was working in my office, and a broad-shouldered eighth grader named Nathan knocked on my door. I didn't recognize much about him but his sparkly blue eyes. He never spoke much at all back when I had him as a student in the library. He smiled and said, "Sorry to interrupt, I just wanted to give you this." Thinking it was a holiday card, I said thank you. He said good-bye, and I never have seen him again. Yet the envelope he handed me turned into a moment that has defined most of my career since that point. When I opened it, I discovered a one-page handwritten letter in teenage-boy scrawl. He began by saying, "You probably don't remember the day you told our class about *Holes*. But I remember." He went on to tell me that the way I talked about that particular book on that particular day struck him like a thunderbolt. It was the first day he wanted to read. He said he had struggled his whole life up to that point to like reading. He *could* do it, but he didn't want to. Ever. He said that day was the day he turned from a nonreader into a reader, and it changed his life.

He went on to say how well he was doing in middle school and what he was looking forward to doing in high school, and he gave me all the credit.

I do this job for that one chance that what I am showing someone might be the right book at the right time for the right person. I connect books with kids, and that is the best part about my job.

His letter is in my bedside nightstand, where it has remained for nine years!

Q: **What's the worst part of your job?**

A: Not enough time or resources to do all that I would like to do for kids. Oh, and paper cuts.

EUREKA!
You Gotta Meet a Scientist!

Think of a scientist.

Did you picture a man in a lab coat holding up test tubes of smoking liquid? It's a common characterization, but one that is quickly dispelled once you spend some time with one. First off, not all scientists work in labs. Some are teachers who work in colleges, high schools, and maybe even your school. Your veterinarian is a scientist, as are your dentist, doctor, and pharmacist. The people who design roller coasters and computers  are scientists, and so are those who test food and products for companies. Of course, they are also the people who study our planet, the living things that inhabit it, and the whole rest of the universe. Scientists are invariably curious, and most would love to talk to anyone who shares an interest in the world around them. If that's you, introduce yourself to a scientist as soon as possible!

Strategies

- Talk to your science teacher! If he or she is a scientist, you're all set. If not, ask if they can get you in contact with one.
- Research the companies or organizations that may employ scientists and see if you can visit where they work.
- Join a local astronomer's club, nature organization, or animal preserve or zoo. Meet the scientists who work there and get to know them.

Ask Away

- What do you study?
- When did you know you wanted to be a scientist?
- What do you think is the most amazing unanswered question that you would love to answer?
- What's your advice for kids who want to be scientists?

SOME FAMOUS SCIENTISTS

MARIE CURIE
NIKOLA TESLA
JANE GOODALL
NEIL DEGRASSE TYSON

Check It Out

Great science site for kids: www.tryscience.org
Lots of great science links: sciencespot.net/Pages/kidzone.html
Science news: www.sciencenewsforkids.org

"The best scientist is open to experience and begins with romance—the idea that anything is possible."—Ray Bradbury

BURNING CALORIES, NOT FOSSIL FUELS
You Gotta Meet an Alternative Transporter!

We spend a lot of time in our cars—going to work, school, soccer practice, the doctor, etc. That's more time sitting around after sitting all day at your school desk! Some people refuse to drive or hardly drive at all. They ride, skate, scooter, and board to work, school, the movies, the grocery store, and their friends' houses. With the right gear and the rules of the road in mind, these energy-conscious people make a point of burning a different kind of fuel—calories instead of gas—while changing their communities' ideas about how to best get from one place to another. Some of these transporters are also activists, working to make the roads safer for cyclists and other nondrivers. Getting in shape while protecting the environment—not a bad deal!

Strategies

• Check around for clubs for people who ride to work or school.
• Does anyone in your class ride or walk to school? See if you can get a group together to travel to school using your own power.

Ask Away

- How do you spread the word about what you do?
- How can kids avoid "driving" to school and activities?
- What do you do when it rains or snows?

Check It Out

Example of a local alternative mode of transportation: *ashevilleonbikes.com*

News and tips for bikers: *www.commutebybike.com*

Type in your address and find out how walkable your neighborhood is: *www.walkscore.com*

"Bicycling is a big part of the future. It has to be. There's something wrong with a society that drives a car to work out in a gym." —Bill Nye

Many cities around the world have bicycle-sharing systems in which free bicycles are provided for people wanting to get around without having to use their cars. You simply pick up a bicycle at a station and return it to another one when you're done.

Did You Know?

A Danish study found that kids who walked or rode their bikes to school could concentrate better in the classroom than kids who took the train or were driven.

MEET MiKE SULE, TEaCHER, aCTiViST, aND aCTiVE TRaNSPORTER!

Mike is from Longport, New Jersey, but he makes his home in Asheville, North Carolina, where, even though most people there drive cars to get where they need to be, Mike rides his bike . . . rain or shine!

Q: **What does it mean to be an alternative transporter?**

A: For me, the alternative transporter is the user of the automobile. People walk before they drive, so walking is really the primary mode, and cycling the secondary. When talking about walking, bicycling, and transit use, I prefer the term *active transportation*. When people engage in active transportation, they change how they interact with the world.

Q: What are some of the benefits of active transportation?

A: Well, it puts people in real settings. Biking and walking are ways for us to reconnect with people and places. We live in a hectic world, and active transportation affords us a few precious moments to be grounded.

Q: Why do you ride your bike instead of drive to work?

A: There are so many reasons why I ride, from economic to health to environmental. I save roughly $10,000 a year by not owning a car. I'm in excellent health. And biking is one way to take ownership of the environmental challenges we face. To be honest, though, the primary reason I ride is simply because I enjoy it. I'm really lucky that I begin each day participating in my favorite activity.

Q: How do you spread the word about what you do?

A: I just follow the Cat in the Hat's mantra: "It's fun to have fun, but you have to know how." People are always excited to have fun, so I just build on the premise that bicycling is fun. I also work to add a social component to riding. I love hosting group rides so that people have a chance to connect as they roll about the city. Biking is social and a bit adventurous, so it really resonates with people.

Q: How can kids avoid "driving" to school and activities?

A: This is a big challenge because so many of our roads are designed for cars. Walking and biking have been left out of our understanding of transportation, and all too often it's not practical for students to walk or ride.

Beyond advocating for complete streets at the city, state, and national level, I think there is a

powerful connection between transit, biking, and walking. I encourage students to learn how to use our city bus system. It's simple enough. I also encourage them to consider the hassle and expense of driving and compare it with the cost and ease of use of transit. Our buses are equipped with bicycle racks, so it's easy to access some great places to pedal via bus. Transit can also be a very social activity for kids. They can text while on the bus with very low risk of serious consequences! The same cannot be said about driving.

Q: How can schools help?

A: Our schools teach drivers' education, and I'd really like to expand on that. I think students would benefit from transportation education. Why aren't we teaching students how to use crosswalks, how to use transit maps, and how to be safe bicyclists? We teach how to drive without much emphasis on the other options.

Q: How do you carry all your stuff with you to work?

A: I have a rack on the back of my bike with bags that hold my stuff for work, a change of clothes, and my lunch. The Internet really makes commuting by bike easier, as documents can be saved on flash drives or in the cloud.

Q: What do you do when the weather doesn't cooperate?

A: Ride through it! After eight years of riding full-time, I have the gear and the systems in place to arrive at my destination comfortably. When people are just getting into riding, I tell them it's okay to continue to drive. Riding a bicycle isn't an all-or-nothing situation. A cold, rainy morning can be a challenge, so if a person isn't prepared to pedal, don't. Take the bus, carpool, or drive. There are plenty of other options.

CAN OPENERS FOR THE MIND
You Gotta Meet a Teacher!

This one may sound easy since you meet teachers all the time. But how much do you *really* know about your teachers? What do they like to do when they're not hounding you to do your homework? Why did they decide to become teachers in the first place? You spend seven or more hours a day, 180 days a year with your teachers, and if you stop to think about it, you may find that you know very little about them.

Strategies

- Stay after school, especially if your teacher has a club he or she sponsors. In this smaller setting, you may learn a lot more about your teacher as a person.
- Invite a teacher to dinner.
- If you find that your teacher shares a common interest with you (reading, astronomy, whatever!), bring it up during recess or after school.
- Start a reading or movie group with your teacher where whoever wants

to join reads the same book or watches the same movie and then meets to talk about it.
- Do a series of profiles of your school's teachers. Post the essays on your school's website.

Ask Away

- What's your favorite book?
- What's your favorite part of your job? What's your least favorite?
- If you weren't a teacher, what other job would you like doing?
- Who was your favorite teacher growing up? Why?

SOME FAMOUS TEACHERS

Jaime Escalante
Annie Sullivan
J. K. Rowling
Frank McCourt

Check It Out

Fun site all about teachers:

www.teacher-appreciation.info

Watch videos on some famous teachers:

bit.ly/14RROGp

Education through the ages:

bit.ly/XUnuYB

"We teachers are rather good at magic, you know." —J. K. Rowling

FUN Fact

GENE SiMMONS OF THE ROCK BAND KiSS WaS FiRED FROM HiS TEACHING POSiTION FOR TEACHING SPiDER-MaN COMiCS iNSTEaD OF SHaKESPEaRE.

FiVE FiCTiONaL TEACHERS WE WiSH WERE REaL!

ALBUS DUMBLEDORE
YODa
MS. FRiZZLE
MS. HONEY
iNDiaNa JONES

THE BOSS
You Gotta Meet a CEO!

Every business needs to have a plan to get and remain successful. The person in charge of this plan is the top boss, often known as the chief executive officer (CEO). Famous CEOs write books or even have movies made out of their careers, but the CEOs in your town probably don't make headlines, even though their jobs are often difficult and demanding. Whether running a bank, a large corporation, or a small Internet startup, the CEO manages the company, provides leadership for employees, hires people to help carry out the business, and offers a long-term plan that will help the company meet and exceed its goals.

Strategies

- Identify the companies in your town and start making inquiries. Once you've identified a CEO you'd like to meet, ask if she or he would be willing to visit your school.
- Read the local newspaper and look for information on CEOs making the news.
- Reach out to local business organizations.
- Research who is on your school's board; there might be some CEOs already working for your school!

Ask Away

- What was your first job and how did it prepare you for your job now?

- What is the most challenging part of your job?
- What, in your opinion, does someone need in order to be a great leader?
- Who influenced you the most as a child?

Check It Out

A list of the world's most powerful women, including many CEOs:
www.forbes.com/power-women/list

List of CEOs of major companies: bit.ly/10iDZO

Play the CEO game: www.ceoonline.com/business_game.aspx

"Leadership is hard to define, and good leadership even harder. But if you can get people to follow you to the ends of the earth, you are a great leader."—Indra Nooyi

SOME FaMOUS CEOs

Laura Lang
Jack Welch
Mark Zuckerberg
Indra Nooyi

TREE HUGGERS AND WORLD SAVERS
You Gotta Meet an Environmentalist!

An environmentalist is anyone who changes his or her life habits in order to improve and protect the Earth's natural environment. That can mean private things, like composting kitchen scraps, driving an electric car, buying local produce, or turning off unneeded lights, or public things, like protesting the government's inaction on environmental issues, working to turn companies more green, and speaking up about green issues. Each community needs to step up and reduce its carbon footprint so that there's plenty of Earth's beauty and nourishment left for future generations, and meeting the environmentalists in your neighborhood will help you get started on your own green journey.

Strategies

- Ask your neighbors and friends what they do to help the environment.
- Research local blogs that focus on environmental issues in your community.
- Attend town or city council meetings.
- Research green companies in your neighborhood and ask someone there for an interview.

Ask Away

- What do you do to reduce your carbon footprint?
- How difficult is it to go green?
- How can our community become more environmentally friendly?
- Which alternative energy sources do you think hold the most promise for our future needs?

Check It Out

Great documentary: *noimpactman.typepad.com*
A short video about consumption: *www.storyofstuff.org*
All about going green: *www.treehugger.com*
Global Green USA's site: *www.globalgreen.org*

"The more clearly we can focus our attention on the wonders and realities of the universe about us, the less taste we shall have for destruction." —Rachel Carson

SOME FAMOUS ENVIRONMENTALISTS

ED BEGLEY, JR.
COLIN BEAVAN
RACHEL CARSON
SEVERN CULLIS-SUZUKI

FUN FACT

IN 2009, COLIN BEAVAN AND HIS WIFE AND DAUGHTER TRIED TO LIVE A CARBON-NEUTRAL LIFE FOR A FULL YEAR—IN THE MIDDLE OF NEW YORK CITY. THE DOCUMENTARY OF THEIR ADVENTURE IS CALLED NO IMPACT MAN.

ENVIRONMENTAL GLOSSARY

- alternative energy: a form of energy to use in place of oil and gas
- carbon footprint: a measure of the impact a human's activities have on the environment in terms of the amount of greenhouse gases produced, measured in units of carbon dioxide
- carbon neutral: achieving net-zero carbon emissions or avoiding emitting any greenhouse gases
- global warming/climate change: the rise in the average temperature of Earth's atmosphere and oceans due to human activity
- greenhouse gases: gases that trap heat in our atmosphere, raising the temperature
- locavore: a person dedicated to eating food grown and produced locally

TO THE RESCUE
You Gotta Meet a Firefighter!

The news is filled with stories of firefighters putting out fires in cars and homes, saving people in dangerous situations, and arriving first on the scenes of accidents. In other words, a firefighter is definitely someone you *want* to meet but don't want to *need* to meet!

Firefighters usually work in companies out of a firehouse. Their shifts range in duration, but often they will work for a full day and sleep and eat at the house, waiting to be called to action. You can meet firefighters at their firehouses, and if you tell them ahead of time you'd like to visit, they may be able to show you the equipment and the different fire trucks. When you visit, bring them a small token of appreciation for all they do for your community.

Strategies

- Help your teacher organize a class trip to the fire station. Just be prepared to cut the visit short if a call comes in!
- Invite a firefighter to come to your class to show off some of his or her equipment, talk about fire safety, and tell stories.

SOME FAMOUS
FIREFIGHTERS

PAUL REVERE
MOLLY WILLIAMS
BRIAN WILLIAMS
ROSEMARY BLISS

Ask Away

- How do you feel when you first hear the fire alarm go off in the firehouse?
- How much training do you do each week?
- Do you really save kittens stuck in trees?

Check It Out

The history of women in firefighting: *bit.ly/Py1OMd*
The International Association of Fire Fighters: *www.iaff.org*
An article about firefighters: *bit.ly/gwLpfX*
All about fire safety: *www.firefacts.org*

"What is a firefighter? He's the guy next door . . . Yet he stands taller than most of us."—author unknown

BRINGING THE PAST TO LIFE
You Gotta Meet a Historical Reenactor!

Historical reenactors are the closest things we have to time travelers (as long as you want to travel *back* in time)! Reenactors come together in costume to recreate some of history's most interesting moments, from ancient Roman times and the Middle Ages to the Civil War, World War II, and more. Different groups represent different time periods or people. Some groups participate in battles, often reenacting famous moments from wars, while others demonstrate different aspects of everyday life. However, they all share a love of history and the many nuances and details that, when woven together, made a huge impact on the world as we know it.

Strategies

- Research local reenactment groups on the Internet and look for reenactment announcements in your local newspaper.
- Check with local museums to see if they have any reenactment activities.
- Most reenactment groups have websites with information, including the events that they participate in and videos and photographs of past events.

Ask Away

- How does one become a historical reenactor?
- How much preparation do you need in order to be part of the reenactment?
- Do you play a specific character? If so, who are you?
- Where did you get your uniform?
- What's the best way to find out if there are any historical reenactments in my hometown?
- Are all reenactments battles or do you do other historical moments?

Check It Out

The home of reenacting: www.reenactor.net
A primer on reenacting: bit.ly/10j8Dpj
A famous reenactor: www.georgecuster.com

SOME FAMOUS HISTORICAL REENACTORS

STEVE ALEXANDER
MAX AND DONNA DANIELS
RALPH ARCHBOLD
CHARLIE SCHROEDER

A WORD OR TWO FROM MY FRIEND CRAIG CHENEVERT, A HISTORICAL REENACTOR

"I belong to an eighteenth-century militia group that participates in both battle and living history events, recreating things that took place in the years leading up to the American Revolution. The Boston area, where I live, played a significant role in the early history of the country, and I have many opportunities to commemorate the historic events that took place. My militia group gathers often to practice for upcoming events.

"Reenactors refer to their clothing and accessories as *kits*, which must adhere to strict guidelines that ensure historical accuracy. I hand-sew my clothes using authentic patterns and fabrics. I also purchase authentic reproductions for items such as shoes and hats and follow the standards established by my militia unit about how I must act when representing the group.

"During battle reenactments, I enjoy the camaraderie that the original militias must have felt walking the same roads with their neighbors and friends. Encampments allow reenacting groups to share their knowledge and skills with the public. We perform the routine drills that the original militia performed as part of their responsibilities as citizens. Some members of the group discuss the historical significance of our group in the Revolutionary War. Others demonstrate cooking and sewing techniques. I share my leather-working skills and display leather water bottles, saddlebags, and cartridge boxes that I have made. We also participate in living history events. I might be a guide or an actor or simply wander about, maintaining my eighteenth-century persona. And maybe best of all, occasionally, I get to march in parades!"

WON'T TAKE IT SITTING DOWN
You Gotta Meet an Activist!

Activism means noticing something wrong in your community, nation, or world and taking action. It's about trying your best to make a difference and change whatever it is that you believe is harmful. Some activists write letters to politicians telling them their laws don't work. Some give speeches, create posters, organize protests, and march in demonstrations in order to spread the word and demand change. Others create art, articles, novels, photographs, dances, and music for their causes. Activists want justice for oppressed people around the world, they work to stop cruel animal testing that companies and laboratories perform, they march to let everyone know that our natural environment needs protection, and more. Activists come in all shapes and sizes, but most aren't afraid to be loud and impassioned. Some also aren't afraid to get into trouble with the law and will even allow themselves to be arrested for demonstrating illegally.

Strategies

- Read or watch the news for any upcoming protests or demonstrations. With a responsible adult, decide whether or not the protest will be peaceful, safe, and legal, and plan on attending. You'll run into all sorts of people at demonstrations, but if you want to meet the organizers, listen to the people giving speeches, talking into bullhorns, and handing out literature. Approach one of them and ask if they'd be willing to talk to you

or visit your school (get your teacher's or principal's permission first).

- If a demonstration feels a bit too chaotic for you, check to see if the organizers have any other events you can attend, such as debates, speeches, or art viewings.
- Read up on the cause of any demonstration before attending a meeting or event. If you don't agree with its purpose, you might want to skip it.
- Activists want to spread the word. Turn your conversation into an article for your school's paper or write an opinion letter to your local newspaper.

Ask Away

- What is your cause and why do you think it's so important to speak up about it?
- How did you first get involved?
- Do you think kids should get involved in activism? Why or why not?
- What's your advice for kids who want to get involved?
- What do people who disagree with you say about your cause?
- Do you ever do anything that could get you in trouble in order to spread the word about your cause?

SOME FAMOUS ACTIVISTS
Rosa Parks
Martin Luther King, Jr.
Ai Weiwei
Julia Butterfly Hill

93

- What do you want the outcome of your protest or demonstration to be?
- How did you find other people who share your ideals?
- What positive changes have you noticed that are the result of your work?

Check It Out

An organization dedicated to teaching kids compassion toward the Earth, people, and animals: www.compassionatekids.com

A cool list of websites for kids looking to take action: *bit.ly/YAl80i*

Facts about activism: *bit.ly/QsnFnZ*

"Never doubt that a small group of thoughtful, committed people can change the world. Indeed, it is the only thing that ever has."—Margaret Mead

NOW, a WORD FROM TAP (TEEN ACTIVIST PROJECT)

"We are members of the Teen Activist Project (TAP). TAP is a group of twenty New York City high school students who see inequality in our communities and want to work to make things better. We meet weekly to learn about civil liberties and legal issues, and we work together to improve our public speaking and community organizing skills. We work hard to make sure the youth of New York know their rights. We help spread the word about issues that matter to us most by talking to our peers, presenting workshops, creating videos, and much more! One piece of advice from us to you is to always speak out for what's right, because in the end we want to make this world a better place!

"Anyone and everyone can be an activist! When they see something is wrong, activists look to take action. A letter, a video, a poster, a song, or even silence, when used correctly, can become a form of activism. Most activists are loud and passionate about what they believe in, and they're not afraid to voice their opinions to the fullest, but there are as many different types of activists as there are people on this planet. If you have a voice or any way to say what you have to say, you can be an activist . . . like us!"

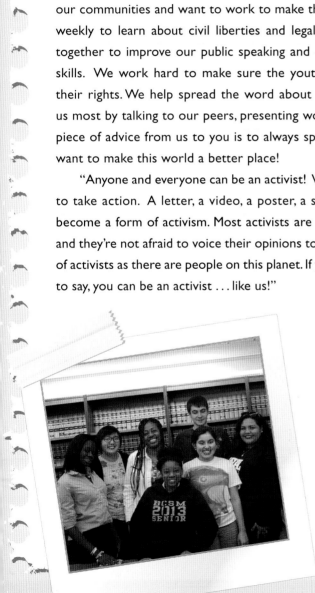

JUST THE FACTS, PLEASE
You Gotta Meet a Journalist!

A journalist (or reporter) is someone who finds noteworthy happenings in your community, across the nation, or around the world, researches and gathers information about them, and then reports them either on television or the radio, in a newspaper or magazine, or online. Journalists cover scientific discoveries, medical breakthroughs, wars halfway around the world, and political squabbles in our nation's capital. They let you know what's up with your favorite celebrities and sports teams, as well as the latest scoop on crime, natural disasters, scandals, human-interest stories, and more. Most journalists adhere to a code of ethics in which they promise to be truthful, accurate, objective (reporting just the facts, without personal opinions), impartial (telling all sides of the story), and fair. That way, when you hear about an important news story, you can make up your own mind how you feel about it.

Strategies

- Journalists are pretty easy to contact, since their jobs depend on interacting with people. Research your local news, free weekly magazines or newspapers, and blogs and choose one reporter whose work you particularly like. Look for his or her e-mail and contact them for a meeting.

- Contact your local newspaper and ask them to send one of their journalists to your school. Turn the tables on the reporter and do a group interview of him or her!

Ask Away

- What's the most interesting or controversial story you ever covered?
- How do you get people to open up and talk to you?
- What's your favorite part of your job?
- Do you feel like our community gets the information it needs to make informed decisions?

Check It Out

Kids reporting for *Time* magazine:
www.timeforkids.com/kid-reporters
News for kids, by kids: bit.ly/1b8WIU
Tips on becoming a journalist: bit.ly/1Z8MDn
A listing of some of the best online places for journalism: journalismdegree.org/best-sites-2012

SOME FAMOUS JOURNALISTS

Jacob Riis
Helen Thomas
Seymour Hersh
Christiane Amanpour

"I believe that good journalism, good television, can make our world a better place."—Christiane Amanpour

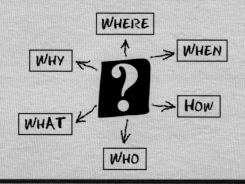

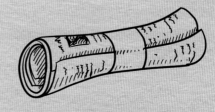

WHERE
WHEN
WHY
?
HOW
WHAT
WHO

MEET MIKE HURLEY. HE'S A JOURNALIST!

Mike covers the Boston sports beat for CBSBoston.com, which is the website for the local CBS TV affiliate and for 98.5 The Sports Hub, the local sports talk radio station. He gets to cover the biggest stories in Boston sports, including the New England Patriots (National Football League), the Red Sox (Major League Baseball), the Bruins (National Hockey League), and the Celtics (National Basketball Association).

Q: How many stories do you cover a week?

A: Writing for a website instead of a newspaper is much different in that we have to cover nearly every story that's been reported pretty much anywhere, so each week I generally have to write about twenty stories. Some of those are quick-hit news items, some come from on-site reporting or feature writing while covering games, and others are written in the style of a traditional newspaper column. The columns are where I have the most fun, as they allow me to express myself, make some arguments, point out some plays or moments that a lot of fans may not have noticed, and occasionally try to be funny. They don't ever come out perfectly, but that's why I keep trying.

Q: What was the most interesting story you've ever covered?

A: That's a tough question, because there have been so many, but one that really stands out is the Boston Bruins' run to the Stanley Cup in the spring of 2011. Each playoff series was so dramatic, with the Bruins playing the hated Canadiens the first round, in the second round getting revenge against the Flyers for a playoff defeat the previous year, battling through seven games against the Lightning in one of the best series I've ever seen, and then beating the highly talented Canucks for the franchise's first championship in thirty-nine years. All of the high-intensity hockey in that two-month period created endless drama each time the team stepped on the ice.

It was also fun because some of the stories I wrote got attention in other parts of the continent, and I ended up being interviewed on the radio in Vancouver and several times in Toronto as well. I didn't really set out to write in order to draw that kind of attention, but when I was chatting hockey for a half hour on the radio in Toronto, which is arguably the center of the hockey universe, it definitely became an instant career highlight for me.

Q: How difficult do you find it to be objective when reporting a story you feel strongly about?

A: I've really never had any problems when it comes to reporting the facts. It's important to be able to keep things fair and right down the middle with a lot of stories, because, as everyone knows, sports fans can get a little crazy sometimes. When reporting the news, I always take it upon myself not to launch them one way or the other, leaving the opinion-making process up to the readers. Now, with that being said, one of the great benefits of my job is that when there is something I have strong opinions about, I am free to express them in my columns. Having that outlet to rant and rave—and occasionally sprinkle in a logical point or two—is the part of my job I most appreciate. It's even better when thousands of people, all with varying opinions on the subject at hand, read my story and chime in with their own thoughts.

Q: What's the most challenging part of your job?

A: Since sports tend to happen at night and on weekends, the schedule can be a bit tiring. It's not unusual to leave a game long after midnight and have to roll into the office early the next morning to get back to work. Plus, while covering games is a treat and an honor, it does limit time spent with family and friends. And there are definitely nights where I'd love to be enjoying a game for what it is rather than sitting quietly behind my laptop in the press row. All things considered, though, it's a small price to pay for being able to have the kind of access to the local sports teams that I always thought would be impossible when I was a kid.

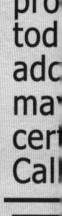

Mike visits with the Stanley Cup—hockey's most coveted prize!

BY HAND
You Gotta Meet a Crafter!

A crafter is someone who makes a product by hand. Crafts harken back to a time when everything was made by hand, from your shoes and clothing to your musical instruments and furniture. Craft pieces are often considered art that you use, and the very best are put on display in museums and art galleries. Crafters often utilize techniques unique to their community that have been passed down through the generations, and many would be happy to talk to someone interested in how they do what they do, if only so their art is passed down to the next generation.

Strategies

- Go to craft fairs and festivals and introduce yourself to the crafters with booths. Chat with them when they're not too busy.
- Find a craft you're interested in and sign up for some classes. Your teacher will not only teach you a new skill, but perhaps also what it means to be a crafter in today's world.

• Visit local arts and crafts studios. Find a stand with crafts that you admire, and if the artist isn't there, take their card and contact them for an interview.

Ask Away

• How long did it take you to learn your craft?
• Do you make your living selling your crafts or is this a hobby?
• How old is your technique?
• Do you think of yourself as an artist? Why or why not?

SOME FAMOUS
CRAFTERS

MARTHA STEWART
SAM MALOOF
SHOJI HAMADA
KATIE BROWN

Check It Out

Site where crafters sell their goods: www.etsy.com
Portland's Crafty Wonderland site: craftywonderland.com/vendors
Great how-to instructions for all sorts of projects: www.instructables.com
A crafting community: craftgrrl.livejournal.com
List of top craft blogs: www.invesp.com/blog-rank/crafts

"You can't use up creativity. The more you use, the more you have." —Maya Angelou

SOME OF THE CRAFTS PEOPLE DO

* bookbinding
* cabinetmaking
* calligraphy
* candle making
* card making
* carpentry
* ceramics

* collage
* doll making
* dressmaking
* felting
* folk art
* glassblowing
* jewelry making

* knitting
* leatherworking
* metalworking
* needlework
* origami
* paper crafting
* papermaking

* pottery
* quilting
* scrapbooking
* shoemaking
* silversmithing
* wood turning
* and more!

SKYLINE BUILDERS
You Gotta Meet an Architect!

Every building in your town or city—every home, apartment complex, strip mall, and skyscraper—needed to be carefully planned out, designed, and built. The person with the technical knowledge and creativity to get this done is called an architect. They not only oversee these complex building projects, but also take into consideration the neighborhoods they're building in, the purposes of the buildings, safety concerns, and aesthetics. In other words, their buildings must be useful, safe, and pleasing to look at. Most communities have local architectural firms that handle a lot of the building design needs, although sometimes firms from elsewhere are hired.

Strategies

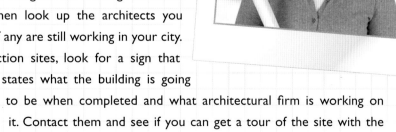

- Look up local architectural firms and see if you can set up an interview.
- Check to see if there are any walking tours of your neighborhood or city. If so, book a tour and ask your guide about the architects who designed the buildings that make up your community. Then look up the architects you learned about and see if any are still working in your city.
- When passing construction sites, look for a sign that states what the building is going to be when completed and what architectural firm is working on it. Contact them and see if you can get a tour of the site with the architect.

Ask Away

- Which buildings in our community have you or your firm designed?
- What's the most difficult part of designing a building?
- What's your favorite building in the world? Why?

Check It Out

The National Building Museum in Washington, DC: *www.nbm.org*
The Center for Understanding the Built Environment: *www.cubekc.org*
The American Institute of Architects: *www.aia.org*

"We shape our buildings, and afterwards our buildings shape us."—Winston Churchill

SOME FAMOUS ARCHITECTS

FRANK LLOYD WRIGHT
JULIA MORGAN
NORMA MERRICK SKLAREK
FRANK GEHRY

FOREVER YOUNG
You Gotta Meet a Senior!

In past cultures, the elderly were revered and valued for their knowledge, wisdom, and advice. You can carry on this vital long-standing tradition by visiting the elderly in your neighborhood. Whether it's a neighbor or someone living in an assisted-care facility or retirement home, you can both benefit from a friendship. You'll provide companionship and perhaps a bright spot in what might be a lonely day. Meanwhile, you'll have an adult who isn't a parent to listen to you, teach you interesting things, and give you advice. You'll be bridging a gap between generations—bringing the past together with the future of your community.

Strategies

- If your school does service work, suggest visiting a retirement home once or twice a month. There you can put on a play, sing, or just hang out. If you want to visit more often, talk to your parents about adopting a grand-friend and plan on visiting after school or on weekends.
- Visit your elderly neighbors; bring them cookies or invite them to dinner. Offer to help

them out with chores, such as putting out the garbage or mowing the lawn. Ask them questions about the neighborhood, where they grew up, and how they feel about the modern world.

Ask Away

- Where and when were you born?
- How are things different today than when you were a kid?
- What are your hobbies?
- What are some of your favorite memories?
- What's your advice for kids growing up today?
- What are some good things about growing older? Bad things?

SOME FAMOUS SENIORS

BETTY WHITE
MAGGIE SMITH
BOB DYLAN
MORGAN FREEMAN

Check It Out

ZOOM helps you help the elderly: *to.pbs.org/4iheo7*

Activities that will help you understand older people better: *bit.ly/12oik9R*

"Don't try to be young. Just open your mind. Stay interested in stuff. There are so many things I won't live long enough to find out about, but I'm still curious about them."—Betty White

THINGS YOU AND YOUR GRAND-FRIEND CAN DO TOGETHER

- take a class together
- do crafts
- share photographs
- play cards
- plant a garden
- discuss your lives
- play with a pet
- talk about what you both did today

VISIT YOUR PARENTS! IT'S THE LAW

ACCORDING TO A LAW IN CHINA, ELDERLY PARENTS WHO FEEL NEGLECTED BY THEIR ADULT CHILDREN CAN SUE THEM. THE CHILDREN CAN BE FINED FOR NOT VISITING REGULARLY.

THE PROBLEM SOLVERS
You Gotta Meet an Engineer!

Engineers are not only mathematicians, scientists, and designers, but also problem solvers and inventors. They know how things work and put that knowledge to use creating new systems, structures, and items that make our lives easier, safer, and more productive. In fact, nearly everything we use was influenced if not directly invented and built by engineers. Some of the most common type of engineers include:

- electrical engineers, who design and build circuits, generators, motors, transformers, complex power systems, etc.
- mechanical engineers, who design and build manufacturing plants, industrial equipment, aircraft, robots, medical devices, etc.
- civil engineers, who build and maintain bridges, canals, lighthouses, etc.
- chemical engineers, who work on large-scale chemical manufacturing
- computer engineers, who develop computer hardware and software

You may not run into too many engineers in your daily life, but we all benefit from their work every day.

Strategies

- Engineers work for all sorts of companies and government departments. With a teacher or parent, come up with a list of businesses that employ engineers. Contact the human resources department of one or more of these businesses and ask them if they can recommend an engineer to meet.
- See if there is a local engineering group you can contact.

Ask Away

- What is a typical workday like for you?
- What led you to become an engineer?
- What inventions do you foresee changing our world in the next twenty years?
- Do you think schools prepare future engineers well? Why or why not?

SOME FAMOUS ENGINEERS

LEONARDO DA VINCI
GRACE MURRAY HOPPER
NIKOLA TESLA
STEVE WOZNIAK

Profiles of engineers: *bit.ly/10jQE1U*

Civil engineering site for kids: *bit.ly/10BB7cv*

Want to become an engineer? *www.earlyengineers.org/index.html*

Magazine that promotes and enhances efforts to improve engineering education: *www.egfi-k12.org*

"Scientists dream about doing great things. Engineers do them."—James A. Michener

SOME OF THE GREATEST ENGINEERING ACHIEVEMENTS

- electricity
- cars
- airplanes
- computers
- telephones
- air-conditioning and refrigeration
- spacecrafts
- the Internet
- health technologies
- lasers

SAY "AHH" You Gotta Meet a Medical Doctor!

We've all had experiences with doctors, either in a hospital or a doctor's office. From birth to death, doctors provide the support we need to lead full and healthy lives. They diagnose illnesses, prescribe medicines and other treatments, perform surgeries, set broken bones, help us work out emotional issues, correct our vision and hearing, and much more. So imagine what it might be like for a doctor to get a visit from someone who isn't sick! Most doctors have visiting hours and may be open to meeting a kid who's interested in what they do and how they go about doing it, although they may only have a few minutes before they're off to help a patient.

Strategies

• The next time you're at the doctor's office for a routine checkup, ask your doctor if they'd be interested in visiting your class or granting an interview.

Rx

PATIENT NAME:
ADDRESS:

DIRECTIONS:

SOME FAMOUS
DOCTORS

Elizabeth Blackwell
Sanjay Gupta
Hippocrates
Sigmund Freud

SIGNATURE:

DATE:

Ask Away

- How long did you have to go to school in order to become a doctor?
- How did you end up practicing the type of medicine you do?
- What advice do you give people who want to get or stay healthy?

Check It Out

What happens when you go to the doctor's office: *bit.ly/ReuR3*

"First, do no harm."—principle of medical ethics

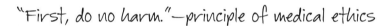

TYPES OF DOCTORS AND THEIR SPECIALTIES

- general or family physician— nonemergency conditions, checkups
- emergency doctor—works in the emergency room of a hospital
- surgeon—performs surgery
- plastic surgeon—cosmetic surgery to repair skin and structural problems
- allergist—allergies
- psychiatrist—mental health
- podiatrist—feet

- orthopedist—bones
- optometrist—eyes
- dentist—teeth
- pediatrician—kids
- oncologist—cancer
- neurologist—brain
- cardiologist—heart
- dermatologist—skin
- veterinarian—animals

NEVER FORGET
You Gotta Meet a Local Historian!

The next time you walk through your town, take a look around you. How did the buildings and shops end up where they are? What was there before them? Who started the town, anyway? As opposed to the history you read in textbooks and watch in documentaries, your community's history may exist chiefly in a few books (depending on where you live) and the people who have made it their job to make sure the stories of your town don't get forgotten. A local historian doesn't have to be elderly, though the best ones have been living in the town long enough to remember a lot of what happened and how things ended up where they did. Some are storytellers who share their love of the past at local festivals; others may be writers, researchers, or building restorers.

Strategies

- See if your town has a local historical society or group. These are formed to save and retell the history of your town, and they are often located in a historic building that they are preserving.
- Ask your librarian if he or she knows of any local historians.
- Look at the community events calendar in your local newspaper for amateur historians giving

talks on a particular part of your town's history. Contact them ahead of time and see if you can set up an interview for after the talk.

- Visit any of your town's historical buildings; local historians may be giving the tours or even working at the gift shop cash register.
- Ask teachers at your school for help finding one.
- Volunteer at a local retirement home. Some of the elderly you meet may have stories that aren't recorded anywhere.

Ask Away

- How long have you lived here?
- What's the most interesting historical fact you've learned about our town?

- Who's the most famous person who's come from here?
- Where can I go to learn more about our town?
- How did you become interested in history?

Check It Out

List of history sites for kids: *bit.ly/dkVvS0* and *bit.ly/Z6TLHO*

"You don't hate history. You hate the way it was taught to you in high school."—Stephen Ambrose

INTERESTED IN YOUR TOWN'S HISTORY? CHECK OUT:

- old local newspapers (check the library or online)
- historical societies
- religious institution records
- census information (at the library)
- *www.ancestry.com*
- Sanborn Maps collection at *sanborn.umi.com* (ask your librarian for help accessing this)
- the Library of Congress Maps Collection at *l.usa.gov/pCGyG*

SOME FAMOUS HISTORIANS

HERODOTUS
DORIS KEARNS GOODWIN
STEPHEN AMBROSE
W. E. B. DU BOIS

DRAWING ON THE FUNNY BONE
You Gotta Meet a Cartoonist!

With a few strokes of the pen, a cartoonist can make you laugh, think, or even question your opinions on things. Cartoonists create drawings that appear in newspapers and magazines as comic strips or editorial cartoons, in books, online, and on TV. Cartoonists, like most artists and comedians, see the world differently, noticing the little things that make people and situations funny, silly, or hypocritical. Meeting a cartoonist can help you not only with your drawing, but also with your ability to pick up on the things that make people laugh and think.

Strategies

- See if there are any cartoons in alternative newspapers in your community. If any of the cartoons refer to local events, there's a good chance the cartoonist is from the area. Find their e-mail and contact them. See if they're interested in doing a school visit or a workshop.
- Check local colleges for cartooning classes or workshops. The instructor will most likely be from your community.

"MY HUSBAND AND I HAVE TALKED FOR YEARS ABOUT HOW WE ALWAYS WANTED TO SEE THE HIMALAYAS! AND THEN THE THOUGHT HIT ME...'WHY NOT JUST INVITE THEM OVER?'"

SOME FAMOUS CARTOONISTS

CHARLES M. SCHULZ
BILL WATTERSON
LYNDA BARRY
WILL EISNER

Ask Away

- Where do you work?
- What kinds of pencils, pens, and paper do you use?
- What are your favorite comics?
- Do you draw for a living?
- How can a kid learn to be a cartoonist?

Check It Out

List of cartoonists: *bit.ly/YAKT0k*

Great cartoons: *www.gocomics.com* and *www.bigblogcomics.com*

Create your own comics: *www.makebeliefscomix.com*

"If I were given the opportunity to present a gift to the next generation, it would be the ability for each individual to learn to laugh at himself."—Charles M. Schulz

MY COLLEAGUE ANTHONY OWSLEY IS a CarTOONIST

Talk about funny! Anthony would love to, especially since it's his job. Born in a small rural community a few miles outside of Knoxville, Tennessee (where most of his neighbors were cows), Anthony now lives in Atlanta, Georgia, with his wife, Stacy. Among many other jobs, Anthony draws cartoons for children's books and for humor magazines such as *Funny Times*. The drawing on pages 116 to 118 are all by Anthony!

Q: What do people do when they meet cartoonists?

A: In real life, whenever people come across a cartoonist, they tend to cross to the other side of the street and protectively cover their children's eyes. (We're not too pretty.)

Q: How did you learn to become a cartoonist?

A: I've been drawing as far back as I can remember. When I was in kindergarten, I would draw comic books about my favorite TV shows and my cats. This was before I even knew how to write. I would show the books to my teacher and dictate to her what words I wanted on the pages. She would write the words where I wanted them and then read my books to the class.

Q: Which cartoonists have influenced you?

A: I was always a big fan of the comic strip *Peanuts*. When I was a kid, I would visit my grandparents every week (their newspaper carried the strip; ours didn't), clip the strips out, and collect them in a scrapbook.

Q: What's the best way to meet you and other cartoonists?

A: Most cartoonists don't go out much because we're always home drawing. Your best bet would be at an art supply store in the aisle with all the drawing pens. We're the ones with black ink stains on our clothes.

Q: How do you come up with funny jokes and gags?

A: A lot of times my ideas will come to me in dreams. I've gotten very good at remembering my dreams and writing them down right when I wake up. Other times, I'll be talking with friends and something funny will pop out and I'll jot it down.

ANIMALS' BEST FRIENDS
You Gotta Meet an Animal Trainer!

People who have a special relationship with animals (as well as years of training!) can help us get along better with our pets by teaching them how to behave properly. They also prepare horses for riding, teach dogs how to guide people with disabilities such as blindness, and more. The most famous animal trainers are often called "whisperers" because of their almost magical relationship with these animals. Even if you don't have a pet, watching a trainer in action can be a rewarding experience.

Strategies

- Visit a dog-training facility or sign your dog up for obedience training. Ask the instructor if they would let you interview them or if they would visit your school.
- Plan a visit to a horse stable or riding center. Ask in the main office to make an appointment with a trainer.
- Ask your veterinarian for a list of local trainers you can contact.

Ask Away

- How did you become an animal trainer? Who influenced you the most?
- What does it take to train a dog (or other animal) successfully?
- What's your favorite thing to do with your animals?
- How can I learn to train my pets?

SOME FAMOUS ANIMAL TRAINERS

BUCK BRANNAMAN
VICTORIA STILWELL
CESAR MILLAN
BOONE NARR

Check It Out

Learn about guide dogs: www.uniteforsight.org/kids/guidedog.php

Watch a video on guide dogs: on.natgeo.com/11y35Zc

"'I'll believe it if I see it' for dogs translates to 'I'll believe it if I smell it.' So don't bother yelling at them; it's the energy and scent they pay attention to, not your words."—Cesar Millan

Dogs and other animals are trained to work with police officers and the military. In this image, a U.S. Navy Marine sergeant works with a trained dolphin, whose job is to locate underwater mines.

MEET MY FRIEND MELISSA HEETER!

Melissa Heeter made history in 1997 when she, with the help of her dog Ariel Asah, became the first woman to win the Canine Disc World Championship. (In this sport, dogs and their owners play toss and fetch with a flying disc for points.) Since then, Melissa has set the outdoor and indoor canine disc distance records and has dedicated her life to teaching pet owners how to have fun, play safely, and strengthen their bonds with their dogs. She lives in Pinconning, Michigan.

Q: What does an animal trainer do?

A: The main goal of an animal trainer is to help pet owners understand how to communicate with their pets while strengthening their relationship.

Q: How did you become an animal trainer? Who influenced you the most?

A: Growing up on a farm in Michigan was an exciting adventure, training horses, dogs, and so many other farm animals. My father was my idol and influenced me the most on how important it was to create a trusting relationship with your animals.

121

Q: **What does it take to train a dog successfully?**

A: Training a dog successfully involves being able to understand how to read a dog's body language and how a dog learns. The successful loyal friendships come through trust, exercise, and leadership.

Q: **What's your favorite thing to do with your pets?**

A: One of my favorite activities is a simple game of fetch by throwing a flying disc for my dog.

Q: **How can I learn to train my pets?**

A: One of the most successful ways for pet owners to train their dogs is to work in short sessions using a positive reinforcement method. The best way to find the most effective way for you to train your own dog is to find a dog trainer in your area who is successful in the type of training you want to accomplish with your dog.

HAVE YOU TWO MET?
You Gotta Meet Yourself!

Whether you know it or not, you're an integral part of your neighborhood. And even though you've already "met" yourself, how well do you *know* yourself? Are you loud and passionate when arguing about issues that you care about? Do you like to draw, write, cook, sculpt, or otherwise create? Do you enjoy working with people or with animals? Do you like helping others? By meeting with as many of the people who make your community what it is as possible, you are not only learning about the world, but also about yourself and your place within the community today and in the future. Let the people you learn about here help you learn more and more about what makes you you.

Strategies

- Keep a journal and write down your random thoughts, ideas, dreams, and more.
- Write interview questions for yourself and record the interview.
- Make lots of lists.
- Create an imaginary conversation or interview with your ninety-nine-year-old self.
- Meditate.
- Take a personality quiz.

123

Ask Away

- What do you want to be when you grow up?
- Who in this book inspires you the most? Why?
- How do you want to contribute to your community?
- Do you want to be famous? Why or why not?
- What questions do you have for the author of this book? His e-mail is joe@joerhatigan.com.

Check It Out

Journal prompts: *bit.ly/PcDxs5*
Personality quizzes: *bit.ly/dbwq5q* and *bit.ly/Y393x3*
Meditation techniques: *bit.ly/SVthZS*

SOME FaMOUS YOUS
THERE'S NO ONE QUITE LIKE YOU!

"Know yourself . . . know the world."
—Me, Joe Rhatigan

And have fun!!!

Acknowledgments

The author would like to thank the following for their assistance with this fun and challenging project. Without these people, this book would have been even more challenging and a lot less fun: Mark & Monica Bastin, Sara Bogan, Jennifer Carnig, Craig Chenevert, Jennifer Coleman, Tom Downing, Lauren Frederico, Li'l Baby Gerber, Melissa Gerber, Kelly Milner Halls, Melissa Heeter, Kate Hurley, Mike Hurley, Charlie Nurnberg, Jeremy Nurnberg, Anthony Owsley, Maya Penn, Dan Phillips, Rolf Potts, Kayleigh Rhatigan, Kevin Smith, Mike Sule, the Teen Activist Project, C. Michael Walsh, and Aidan Weaver.

Photo Credits

Index